WORLD FACT FILES

Ecuador Peru Bolivia

Edward Parker

MACDONALD YOUNG BOOKS

First published in 1998 by Macdonald Young Books
An imprint of Wayland Publishers Ltd
© Macdonald Young Books 1998

Macdonald Young Books
61 Western Road
Hove
East Sussex
BN3 1JD

Find Macdonald Young Books on the Internet at
http://www.wayland.co.uk

Design and typesetting Roger Kohn Designs
Commissioning editor Hazel Songhurst
Editor Merle Thompson
Assistant editor Diana Russell
Picture research Shelley Noronha
Maps János Márffy

We are grateful to the following for permission
to reproduce photographs:
Front Cover: J Horner *above*;
Getty Images *below* (Ed Simpson);
B Coleman, page 43 (Gunter Ziesler); Getty Images, pages
10/11 (Kevin Schafer), 11 *below* (Robin Smith); Robert
Harding, page 37; Jeremy Horner, page 39 *below*; Image
Bank, page 18 (P & G Bowater); Impact, pages 20 *above*
(Michael Mirecki), 22 *right* (Colin Jones), 24 (Michael Mirecki),
27 (Piers Cavendish), 28 (Robert Gibbs), 35 *left* (Robert
Gibbs), 38 (Alastair Indge), 45 (Robert Gibbs); Tony Morrison,
pages 9, 12 *above*, 13, 14, 19 *above* and *below*, 20 *below*, 30
above (Robert Francis), 30 *below*, 41 *above*; NHPA, page 40
(Kevin Schafer); Edward Parker, pages 8 *above* and *below*, 12
below, 15 *above* and *below*, 16, 17, 21, 22 *left*, 23, 25 *above*
and *below*, 31, 32 *left*, 32/33, 34 *left*, 35 *right*, 39 *above*, 44
above; Rex Features, page 29 *left* (Wesley Bocxe); Still
Pictures, pages 26 *above* and *below*, (Mark Edwards), 29
above (John Maier), 36 (Mark Edwards), 41 *below* (Mark
Edwards), 44 *below* (Chris Caldicott); Harry Trusted, page 43.

The statistics given in this book are the most up to date
available at the time of going to press

Printed in Hong Kong by Wing King Tong

A CIP catalogue record for this book is available from
the British Library

ISBN: 0 7500 2436 4

CONTENTS

Words that are explained in the glossary are printed in
SMALL CAPITALS the first time they are mentioned in the text.

INTRODUCTION

Ecuador, Peru and Bolivia lie on the western side of South America. Together they cover almost 2.7 million square kilometres, or around 15% of the continent's total land area: a quarter of the size of the USA and 10 times as big as the UK.

If you ask people what they know about these countries, some may mention the ancient Inca civilization. Others will speak of local people playing haunting pan-pipe music. Many will talk of the soaring, snow-capped Andes mountains, steamy tropical forests and baking deserts. They may also mention the severe social problems and turbulent political history of the region. However, there is much more than this to these countries, which each have their own distinct character.

Long before the first Europeans arrived here, great civilizations developed in the region. Between 1400 BC and AD 1532, many cultures flourished, such as the Nazca of the Peruvian desert, the Tiahuanaco-Huari of the highlands of Bolivia, and the Incas.

The Incas built large cities, massive stone temples and palaces, and a major network of roads. Theirs was a highly organized society. At its peak, the Inca empire stretched north beyond Ecuador into Colombia, and south and east through Bolivia into Chile and Argentina.

In the 16th century, rumours of gold and other riches attracted the Spanish to the area. They

▲ *This stone carving of a warrior belongs to the Chavin culture, which flourished on the western slopes of the Andes between 1300 and 400 BC.*

▲ *Around half the population of all three countries continue to live in the Andes, growing their food in gardens such as this one in Ecuador.*

conquered the Incas and ruled here for around 300 years. After a violent colonial history, all three countries fought for and gained independence from Spain in the early 19th century.

Today Ecuador, Peru and Bolivia are countries of great contrasts. In each one, there are wealthy and cosmopolitan cities, but there are also areas where many people live in conditions of great poverty, with few schools and hospitals.

You can find out about all these aspects of the region in this book.

▼ *La Paz is the capital of Bolivia and the highest capital city in the world. Its central plaza stands at an altitude of 3,636 metres. The snow-covered peak of Mount Illimani (6,402 metres) towers over the city.*

ECUADOR, PERU AND BOLIVIA AT A GLANCE

● Population density: 38.4 people per square kilometre in Ecuador, 18.7 in Peru, 7.2 in Bolivia
● Largest cities (1990–93): Lima 5.71 million; Guayaquil 1.76 million; Quito 1.29 million; La Paz 715,000; Santa Cruz 700,000; Callao 640,000; Arequipa 619,000; Trujillo 509,000
● Highest mountain: Huascarán (Peru), 6,768 metres
● Longest river: Amazon 6,516 kilometres (of which 3,419 kilometres are wholly within the region)
● Main languages: Spanish, Quechua, Aymara
● Major religions: Roman Catholicism, traditional beliefs
● Major resources: Fish, timber, silver, copper, lead, tin, oil, gas
● Major products: FISHMEAL, oil, bananas, shrimps, coffee, fruit, cotton, textiles, timber, minerals
● Environmental problems: Soil erosion, DEFORESTATION, water and atmospheric pollution

THE LANDSCAPE

The region formed by Ecuador, Peru and Bolivia has a very varied landscape. It includes mountains covered in snow, tropical beaches, parched deserts, luxuriant rainforests and bleak, windswept plateaux.

Peru and Bolivia lie south of the Equator, which cuts across Ecuador just north of the capital, Quito. Peru and Ecuador are bordered on the west by the Pacific Ocean, while Bolivia has no coastline. The region has frontiers with Colombia, Brazil, Paraguay, Argentina and Chile.

The three countries stand on a part of the

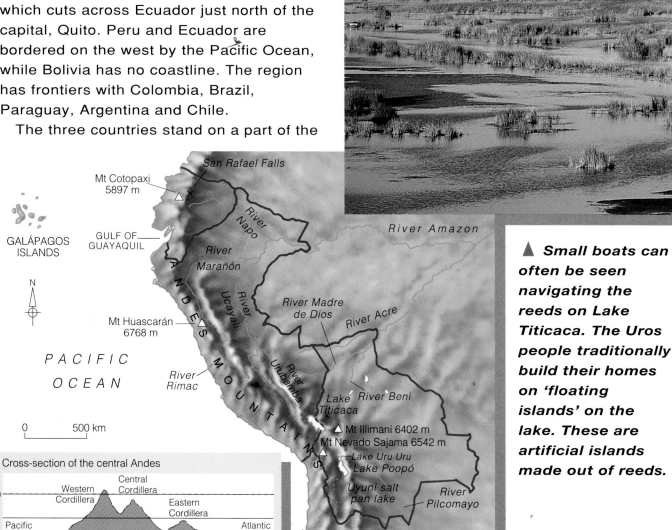

GALÁPAGOS ISLANDS

GULF OF GUAYAQUIL

San Rafael Falls

Mt Cotopaxi 5897 m

River Napo

River Amazon

River Marañón

River Ucayali

River Madre de Dios

River Acre

Mt Huascarán 6768 m

ANDES MOUNTAINS

PACIFIC OCEAN

River Rimac

River Urubamba

River Beni

Lake Titicaca

Mt Illimani 6402 m
Mt Nevado Sajama 6542 m

Lake Uru Uru
Lake Poopó

0   500 km

Uyuni salt pan lake

River Pilcomayo

Cross-section of the central Andes

6000 m

Western Cordillera

Central Cordillera

Eastern Cordillera

3000 m

Pacific Ocean

Atlantic Ocean

▲ *Small boats can often be seen navigating the reeds on Lake Titicaca. The Uros people traditionally build their homes on 'floating islands' on the lake. These are artificial islands made out of reeds.*

earth's crust where there is a GEOLOGICAL FAULT. This means that there are many volcanoes here, and large earthquakes hit the region several times a century.

The region is dominated by the Andes mountain range, which runs approximately north-east to south-west. The Andes are

made up of 'cordilleras', or ranges, which are roughly parallel to one another. In Peru, there are three: the Western, Central and Eastern Cordilleras.

The Andean region gradually widens as you travel south. Only 100 kilometres wide in Ecuador, the range is 300 kilometres wide by the time you reach Bolivia. Many

peaks are over 6,000 metres high.

Between the mountain ranges are the high plains known as 'puna' or, around Lake Titicaca, ALTIPLANO. They are 3,000 to 4,500 metres high. These areas are well suited to agriculture and are the traditional home of the rural Andean population. Only in the very south of Bolivia do the high fertile valleys give way to deserts.

Ecuador's coastline consists of a narrow belt of low-lying land, covered in tropical vegetation. It is no more than 100 kilometres at its widest. An even narrower strip of land forms Peru's coastal region between the Andes and the Pacific. Rarely more than 50 kilometres wide, it is a barren desert punctuated by only 50 small OASES along

► *The western slopes of the Andes in Peru are rugged deserts where little is able to grow, apart from cacti.*

KEY FACTS

● Peru's Colca Canyon is the world's deepest canyon (over 2,000 metres) – twice as deep as the Grand Canyon in the USA.
● Lake Titicaca is the world's highest navigable lake (3,805 metres).
● At 5,897 metres, Cotopaxi (Ecuador) is the highest active volcano in the world.

its entire 2,400-kilometre length.

The eastern sectors of all three countries are covered by lowland tropical rainforest. This accounts for two-thirds of Bolivia's total land area. These lands have very low population densities.

South America's longest river, the Amazon, has its source in Peru close to the Pacific coast, but flows more than 6,000 kilometres east across Brazil to the Atlantic. Only 3,419 kilometres actually pass through Peru. The longest river that flows entirely through the region is the Ucayali (1,771 kilometres).

Ecuador's longest river is the Napo, which forms one of the Amazon's principal northern TRIBUTARIES.

Bolivia has two great river systems. One is the River Pilcomayo, which flows south into Paraguay, where it joins the River Paraguay. The other is formed by ten major rivers, including the Acre, Madre de Dios and Beni, which flow north, draining into the Amazon basin. The largest lake in the region is Lake Titicaca, covering an area of 8,135 square kilometres on the frontier between Peru and Bolivia.

▶ *The spectacular 145-metre San Rafael Falls in the eastern foothills of the Andes. This is Ecuador's largest waterfall. It is surrounded by rainforest.*

◀ *Destruction caused by an earthquake in the town of Baeza, Ecuador, in 1987. All three countries suffer from earthquakes and volcanic eruptions.*

CLIMATE AND WEATHER

The region lies mainly between the Equator and the Tropic of Capricorn, but its climate is chiefly influenced by two other factors: the altitude of the land, and the ocean currents of the Pacific.

Two currents affect the weather of Ecuador and Peru. One is cold and the

▲ *Covered in snow, Mount Huayna rises up behind llamas grazing on the altiplano grasslands near Potosí, Bolivia.*

other is warm. When the sea is colder than the land, rain falls over the sea; but when the sea is warmer, the coastal areas experience heavy rainfall.

Ecuador is influenced by the warm equatorial counter-current, which creates a hot and rainy season from January to April. There is heavy rain (over 700 mm in the first three months) and it is very hot, averaging more than 30°C. From May to December, the cool Humboldt current from the south dictates the weather. Generally, it is slightly cooler and it rarely rains.

The rainforest area of Ecuador east of the Andes is hot and wet all year, although temperatures are a little lower than those on the coast. However, the Andean region

KEY FACTS

● When EL NIÑO hit Peru in 1993, many areas in the north received 2 metres of rain in 2 months.
● A cold wind from Argentina occasionally blows over Bolivia's lowland rainforest from May to October, reducing temperatures to nearly freezing.
● Between June and August, altiplano areas above 4,000 metres in Peru and Bolivia can have night-time temperatures of -25°C.

itself has a temperate climate, with a dry season between June and September. The highest mountain peaks, such as Cotopaxi, remain snow-capped all year round.

Peru has three distinct climatic zones: the coastal strip, the Andean region and the eastern sector.

In the coastal strip, the weather is controlled by the cold Humboldt current. This ensures that very little rain falls, so most of the coast is a drab and barren desert. During the winter (May to November), a damp mist called the GARÚA rolls over most of the coastal cities, keeping temperatures low at only 13–17°C, compared with 20–26°C in the summer. Every five to ten years, a warm current called El Niño replaces the cold Humboldt current. The effect is devastating. The change from a cold to a warm sea causes

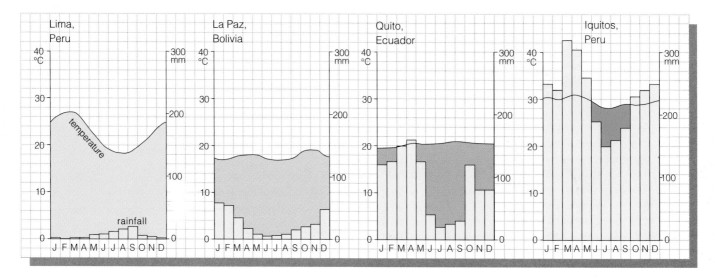

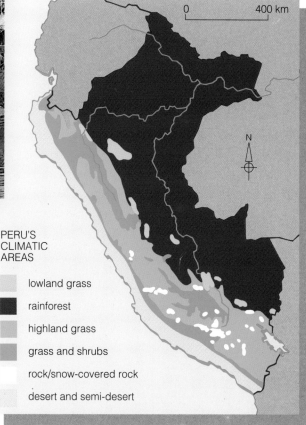

PERU'S
CLIMATIC
AREAS

lowland grass

rainforest

highland grass

grass and shrubs

rock/snow-covered rock

desert and semi-desert

◄ *Peru's coastal strip receives so little rain that very few plants can survive here.*

▲ *A typical coastal village situated along the lush, tropical coastline of Ecuador.*

torrential rains to fall over the desert, rather than out to sea. On the coastal strip, 1,000 mm of rain may fall in less than a month, bringing floods and landslides.

In Peru's Andean region, it is altitude that determines the climate. It is generally temperate in the high valleys, while the higher peaks are always covered in snow. Mountains such as Huascarán have glaciers. By contrast, the country's eastern sector, with its tropical rainforest, is hot and wet all year round.

Bolivia also has a wide range of climatic conditions. Winter frosts occur almost everywhere, even occasionally in the lowland tropical forests. In summer (November to March), there is widespread heavy rain. Around Lake Titicaca, temperatures can quickly fall by 30°C within just a few hours.

However, the country's eastern rainforest is typically humid and hot, with heavy rains for most of the year. The average temperature is close to 25°C and total rainfall is around 3,000 mm a year.

◄ *Heavy rain falling on the town of Pucalpa in Peru's Amazon rainforest means that the streets can quickly become flooded.*

NATURAL RESOURCES

Ecuador, Peru and Bolivia have always been rich in natural resources. An abundance of fish enabled large civilizations to develop along the coast more than 2,000 years ago. Amazonian peoples flourished in the species-rich rainforest. And gold, silver and copper have been mined for over 1,000 years. These metals were used by cultures such as the Chimu, Nazca and Inca to adorn their temples and palaces, and their availability later attracted Europeans to the region.

Minerals are still very important, especially for the economies of Peru and Bolivia. Peru is one of the most important mining countries in the world – it is the third largest producer of silver and the seventh largest producer of copper. The country has big deposits of iron, lead and gold, too. Iron output is the fastest rising sector of the mining economy.

Bolivia also relies heavily on its mineral wealth and the export of metals accounts for 39% of all export earnings. As well as

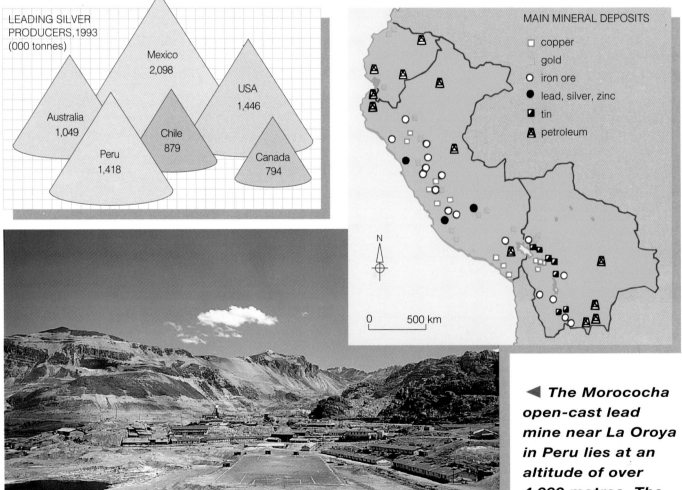

LEADING SILVER
PRODUCERS, 1993
(000 tonnes)

Mexico 2,098
USA 1,446
Australia 1,049
Peru 1,418
Chile 879
Canada 794

MAIN MINERAL DEPOSITS

☐ copper
☐ gold
○ iron ore
● lead, silver, zinc
◩ tin
⛊ petroleum

N

0   500 km

◄ **The Morococha open-cast lead mine near La Oroya in Peru lies at an altitude of over 4,000 metres. The lack of oxygen at this height makes working in the mine difficult.**

lead, zinc and iron, Bolivia has deposits of rare metals such as tin, antimony, tungsten, mercury, silver and gold.

Ecuador does not have the same wealth of metals as Bolivia and Peru, but it does have large oil and gas reserves. Oil and gas were first discovered in 1917 close to the coast. It was not until the 1970s that the large reserves in the Ecuadorean Amazon were first exploited, but oil fields in the rainforested eastern part of the country have now been developed. The oil is transported along the TransAndean pipeline over the Andes to the deep-water port of Esmeraldas. Oil is now Ecuador's largest export, accounting for 39% of all exports.

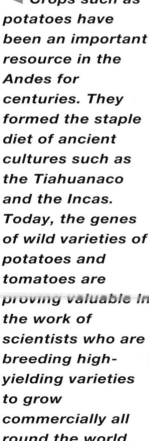

◀ *Crops such as potatoes have been an important resource in the Andes for centuries. They formed the staple diet of ancient cultures such as the Tiahuanaco and the Incas. Today, the genes of wild varieties of potatoes and tomatoes are proving valuable in the work of scientists who are breeding high-yielding varieties to grow commercially all round the world.*

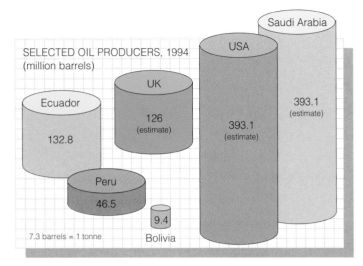

SELECTED OIL PRODUCERS, 1994
(million barrels)

Saudi Arabia

USA

UK

Ecuador

393.1
(estimate)

126
(estimate)

393.1
(estimate)

132.8

Peru

46.5

9.4

7.3 barrels = 1 tonne

Bolivia

Peru has been exploiting relatively small quantities of oil in its northern deserts for many years. More recent exploration in the Amazon rainforest region has led to the discovery of vast oil and gas deposits, including one of the world's biggest fields of natural gas, the Camisea. Extensive FOSSIL FUEL reserves have recently been discovered in the Bolivian rainforest too, and natural gas is becoming one of Bolivia's most important exports.

In the cities, electricity and gas are widely used for fuel. However, a large proportion of the population live in rural locations and rely on firewood for cooking and heating. The rivers coursing down the

 *Exploration for oil and natural gas is being carried out in the rainforest areas of all three countries, using mobile drilling platforms.*

KEY FACTS

● The Camisea gas field near Cuzco in Peru contains an estimated 280 trillion cubic metres of natural gas – 7 times larger than the country's previously known total reserves of oil, gas and coal.
● There are more than 20,000 species of plants in Ecuador, compared with 17,000 in the whole of North America.

steep slopes of the Andes are used to produce electricity and there are many hydro-electricity stations in all three countries. Today these stations produce 53% of Bolivia's electricity, and an estimated 70% in Ecuador.

An unusual mineral deposit found on the islands just off the coast of Peru led to great wealth in the 19th century. This is GUANO, the accumulation of seabird droppings, which is rich in phosphates. Guano is still collected today from the Ballestas Islands just south of Lima. It is used as a fertilizer for local

► *Some tropical hardwoods are very valuable. Bolivia has great potential for timber production – in 1992, exports of sawn timber earned the country US$ 46 million.*

agriculture, although it is less important than it used to be.

Fish are another key local resource for Peru and Ecuador. The coastal waters of Peru form one of the world's most important fisheries, although this can be disrupted by climate conditions.

The eastern areas of all three countries are heavily forested. Products such as rubber, Brazil nuts and quinine (a medicine obtained from the bark of a tree) have been harvested for more than 100 years. However, some areas of the rainforest are being rapidly cut down for logging, cattle ranching and farming, which has led to serious deforestation.

The region's landscapes have become important natural resources for another reason, too. The rugged beauty, and the sheer variety of plants and animals found here, attract people from all over the world, and tourism is becoming increasingly important. However, in some areas such as the Galápagos Islands, 1,000 kilometres off the Ecuadorean coast, tourism has to be restricted to protect the environment.

◄ *One of the boats of the Peruvian anchovy fishing fleet returning to the port of Chimbote. Chimbote is Peru's main fishing port and the centre of the fishmeal industry.*

POPULATION

ORIGINS OF THE POPULATIONS

The modern populations of Ecuador, Peru and Bolivia are descended from the area's INDIGENOUS inhabitants (known as 'Indians') and from Europeans.

The arrival of the Spanish in the 16th century had a dramatic effect on local populations. Millions of indigenous people died of newly introduced diseases such as smallpox, to which they had no resistance. Others died after being forced to work as slaves in mines and on plantations. Bolivia's mercury mines were especially deadly – their toxic fumes meant that miners survived only a few years there.

During the colonial period, which lasted for around 300 years, large numbers of Europeans arrived in the region and cities such as Lima and Quito began to grow rapidly. Many European men married local women. Their descendants are known as MESTIZOS. This group of people now make up 55% of the population in Ecuador, 37% in Peru and 30% in Bolivia.

Small sections of the population are descended from black slaves brought to the area by Europeans to work on the

▲ *Bolivian Indians, wearing their distinctive ponchos and bowler hats, in the crowded city streets of La Paz.*

▼ *These houses in Bolivia are made of stone and adobe (mud-brick) walls. The building techiques used in rural areas today are not very different from those used in Inca times.*

URBAN AND RURAL POPULATIONS, 1993 (%)

urban

58
42

rural
Ecuador

70
30

Peru

55
45

Bolivia

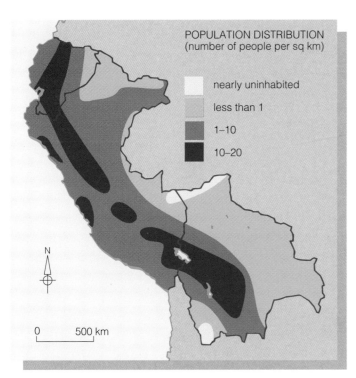

POPULATION DISTRIBUTION
(number of people per sq km)

- nearly uninhabited
- less than 1
- 1–10
- 10–20

N

0   500 km

POPULATIONS OF THE MAIN CITIES

ECUADOR (1990 estimate)		PERU (1993 census)		BOLIVIA (1992 census)	
Guayaquil	1,764,000	Lima	5,710,000	La Paz	715,000
Quito	1,287,000	Callao	640,000	Santa Cruz	700,000
Cuenca	227,000	Arequipa	619,000	Cochabamba	400,000
Machala	166,000	Trujillo	509,000	El Alto	395,000
		Chiclayo	412,000		

accounting for around 55% of the country's total. Most of the indigenous people live on the altiplano and speak either Aymara or Quechua. Similarly, 45% of Peruvians are Indian. But only a quarter of Ecuador's population is Indian. More than half of all Ecuadoreans are mestizo.

In Bolivia and Ecuador, relatively small plantations, and from Chinese people who arrived to work on the railways. At the beginning of the 20th century, thousands of Japanese also migrated to the region.

TODAY'S POPULATIONS

The combined populations of Ecuador, Peru and Bolivia total approximately 43 million people – less than that of the UK, in a region 10 times the size.

The make-up of each country is quite different in terms of population density, ethnic mix and the size of the urban and rural populations. For example, Bolivia has the lowest population density of any country in South America, while Ecuador has the highest figure in the continent.

Bolivia also has the highest Indian population of any South American country,

▶ *The Tsatchila Indians (called 'Colorado' by the Spanish) live in Ecuador's lowland rainforest. They are distinctive because of the red paste they use in their hair.*

numbers of Indians live in the rainforest. However, in Peru the rainforest Indian population is estimated at between 200,000 and 250,000.

MIGRATION

During the 20th century, the populations of all three countries have become much more urban. More than half of all Bolivians and Ecuadoreans now live in towns and cities. In Peru, the figure is around 70%.

Since the 1950s, the extreme poverty experienced by many people in the rural Andes has led to a mass migration towards the coast, especially the cities. Many young people leave the countryside in search of work. This trend increased during the 1970s and 1980s, when terrorist groups such as 'Sendero Luminoso' (Shining Path) were active in the countryside. The migration from the Andes to the coastal cities has slowed since the early 1990s, as terrorist activities have almost ceased in the Andes.

More recently, there has been increasing migration of people from the Andes to the rainforested lowlands. This has been most

◀ *Quito is the second largest city in Ecuador, after the port of Guayaquil. In the old part of the city, people gather at weekends and holidays in squares such as the Plaza Santa Domingo.*

▲ *The river-side houses of Iquitos in the Peruvian rainforest are built on stilts, because water levels here can rise rapidly. Iquitos is Peru's largest rainforest town, and the main commercial centre of the Amazon region.*

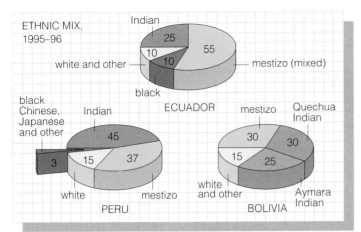

ETHNIC MIX, 1995–96

ECUADOR
- Indian 25
- mestizo (mixed) 55
- black 10
- white and other 10

PERU
- Indian 45
- mestizo 37
- white 15
- black Chinese, Japanese and other 3

BOLIVIA
- mestizo 30
- Quechua Indian 30
- Aymara Indian 25
- white and other 15

notable in Bolivia, where land is being cleared to make way for new plantations and small farms.

POPULATION GROWTH

During the 20th century, the populations of all three countries have grown rapidly.

▶ *Students at a college in Arequipa in Peru reflect the varied ethnic mix of the region's population.*

KEY FACTS

● 45% of Peru's population speak Quechua as their first language, while 25% of people in Bolivia speak Aymara as their first language.

● In 1531, the Inca empire covered a larger area than the Roman empire at its height.

● The region's population density averages just over 16 people per square kilometre – compared with 26 in the USA, 328 in Japan and 620 in Europe.

● Alberto Fujimori, who became President of Peru in 1990, is descended from Japanese migrants who arrived in the country at the beginning of the 20th century.

● The first people to live in the region are thought to have arrived from Asia around 12,000 BC.

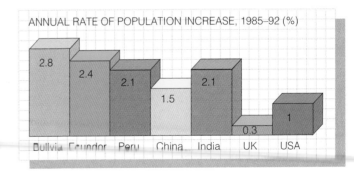

ANNUAL RATE OF POPULATION INCREASE, 1985–92 (%)

Bolivia	Ecuador	Peru	China	India	UK	USA
2.8	2.4	2.1	1.5	2.1	0.3	1

The growth rate is now slowing down: in 1995, Ecuador, Peru and Bolivia had growth rates of 2.3%, 1.9% and 2.0% respectively. However, more than a third of the region's total population is under 15 years of age. This is a high figure compared with the UK (17%) and USA (22%).

DAILY LIFE

FAMILY LIFE

Families in the region are often large. It is quite common for parents, children, cousins and grandparents to live close to one another. Grandparents often help by looking after the children when both parents go out to work. However, the situation is changing as young people leave their home areas in search of work in the cities.

In the cities, many people live in modern apartments; some have expensive houses. However, millions of people continue to live in poverty in the shanty towns around large cities such as Lima, La Paz and Guayaquil. Meanwhile, many indigenous people in the Andes and the Amazon rainforest live in a way that has changed little for centuries.

RELIGION

More than 90% of the three countries' combined population are Roman Catholic.

▲ *Every year in Cuzco, the old capital of the Inca empire, a massive festival called Inti Raymi is held and Andean people celebrate their past.*

MAJOR FESTIVALS AND HOLIDAYS

24 January	ALSITAS (Bolivia; 'Puno' in Peru): festival of abundance that dates from Inca times
February/March (week before Lent)	CARNIVAL: lively celebrations in all three countries
24 May	BATTLE OF PINCHIHCHA DAY (Ecuador): celebrating the decisive battle for independence against the Spanish in 1822
24 June	INTI RAYMI: an Inca festival to the Sun God
24 July	Simón Bolívar's birthday (Ecuador): celebrates the birthday of 'the Liberator'
28 and 29 July	INDEPENDENCE DAY (Peru)
6 August	INDEPENDENCE DAY (Bolivia)
10 August	INDEPENDENCE DAY (Ecuador)
last week of August	CHU'TILLOS (Bolivia): festival in Potosí celebrating traditional music and dance
8 October	BATTLE OF ANGAMOS (Peru)
1 and 2 November	DIA DE TODOS LOS SANTOS: All Saints' Day
24 and 25 December	CHRISTMAS EVE and CHRISTMAS DAY

◀ *Uros Indians on the floating reed islands on Lake Titicaca combine fishing and other traditional activities with selling items to tourists.*

A small percentage are Protestants. However, many people combine Christianity with ancient beliefs. For example, the Apus, or spirits of the mountains, are still revered by Andean Indians. Amazonian Indians also retain many of their groups' traditional beliefs.

LEISURE

As in most Roman Catholic countries, family occasions such as weddings, birthdays and christenings are considered important. Many saints' days are celebrated with processions; some are also marked by national or regional holidays.

In the coastal regions of Peru and Ecuador, people enjoy sunbathing, surfing and even parascending on hot summer days. In the Andes, FIESTAS for family occasions or national holidays are often celebrated in a manner that harks back to Inca times. This includes traditional music and dancing, with a meal where meat is cooked in a PACHA MANCA, an earth oven made by heating up stones.

The most popular sport for men in the region is football. The most popular female sport is volleyball. Televisions are not yet common in the countyside, although watching television is an increasingly popular pastime in towns and cities.

◀ *Office workers enjoy a hot cup of coffee during their lunch hour. This is Miraflores, a wealthy suburb of Lima. Miraflores has many leisure facilities, including shopping malls, cinemas, parks and a beach which is crowded with sunbathers in summer-time.*

► *Many people in La Paz live in slums like this one. In the region, millions have moved from the countryside to the cities in the hope of finding work.*

▼ *Bolivian women queue to buy bottled gas for their cooking stoves. Fuelwood is no longer easy to collect or buy near La Paz.*

SOCIAL PROBLEMS

Peru and Bolivia both have alarming health statistics. In Peru, 47% of children of school age suffer from serious malnutrition. Bolivia's infant mortaltity rate is one of the worst in South America, at 92 deaths per 1,000 live births in 1991, compared with 7 in the UK and 9 in the USA. However, Ecuador's health statistics have shown a rapid improvement over the last 30 years. Between 1960 and 1992, the number of patients per doctor in the country fell from 3,000 to 920. This has helped to raise life expectancy from 56 to 67 years over the same period.

The region faces many serious social problems. The big gap in wealth between the rich and the poor creates a tension that can often lead to violent crime. In Lima, for example, around half the population live in shanty towns, in contrast to the very wealthy who have large mansions with swimming pools and servants.

There are also growing numbers of street children. These are mostly children who

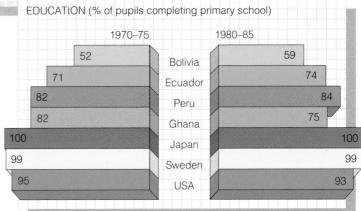

◀ *The school buildings in rural parts of Ecuador, Peru and Bolivia are often very basic – such as this one near Iquitos in Peru. Many remote schools in the rainforest areas are run by missionary organizations.*

have been abandoned to live on their own in the big cities by parents who do not have enough money to bring them up.

One of the most serious problems facing the region is drug trafficking. Peru and Bolivia are the world's largest producers of cocaine. Tonnes of this illegal drug are transported to the USA, Canada and Europe, where addicts are prepared to pay high prices for it.

EDUCATION (% of pupils completing primary school)

	1970–75	1980–85
Bolivia	52	59
Ecuador	71	74
Peru	82	84
Ghana	82	75
Japan	100	100
Sweden	99	99
USA	95	93

KEY FACTS

● Machu Picchu, the lost city of the Incas, was only re-discovered in 1911. It is now the region's top tourist attraction.
● Peru's women's volleyball team is one of the world's best, winning a silver medal in the 1988 Olympics.
● Bolivia's income from the illegal production of cocaine is an estimated 15% of the country's total income.
● Of children who are eligible to enrol for secondary education in Bolivia, only 50% do so.

EDUCATION

Education for children between the ages of 7 and 14 is free and compulsory in all three countries, but many children do not go to school, especially in rural areas. In Bolivia, half of all women living in rural locations cannot read or write, compared with 20% of the population as a whole. The situation is better in Peru and Ecuador, where adult illiteracy stands at around 12%.

The government of Peru has now made education a top priority, spending twice as much money on this in 1995 than was spent in 1990. Peru has 49 universities, attended by 731,000 students.

RULE AND LAW

All three countries were controlled by Spain until the 19th century, when they gained independence. Today, they are all DEMOCRACIES, and since the mid-1980s they have had political stability. However, they have had turbulent histories, with uprisings, military dictators and land disputes.

Bolivia has fared worst in such disputes. It lost much of its territory, including its coastline, to three of its neighbours in wars between 1879 and 1935.

Peru and Ecuador are still in dispute over land in the Amazon rainforest. They went to war over territories in 1941. In 1942 an 'agreement' granted most of the territory to Peru, although Ecuador has never recognized this. The two countries were briefly at war again in 1995.

Under Ecuador's 1978 Constitution, all literate citizens are eligible to vote for a President and Vice-President, who serve four years. The government consists of a single Chamber of 82 members.

In Peru, a new Constitution was approved in 1993. After a five-year term, the

▲ *A statue of Simón Bolívar, 'the Liberator' who fought for independence in the region, standing in the centre of La Paz, Bolivia.*

KEY FACTS

● President Abdula Bucaram of Ecuador (nicknamed 'El Loco') celebrated his election in 1996 by releasing a recording of himself singing 'Jailhouse Rock'.
● In 1996–97, the Tupac Amaru terrorist group held 72 people hostage for 4 months in the Japanese Embassy in Lima, Peru.
● In 1994, the government of Bolivia officially recognized the rights of its indigenous people – for the first time since the Spanish conquest in the 16th century.
● Although it is landlocked, Bolivia has a 4,500-strong navy, based on Lake Titicaca.

KEY HISTORICAL EVENTS	The rise of the first major civilization: the Chavin culture in Peru	Pizarro and the Spanish Conquistadors land on the coast of Ecuador	War of the Pacific: Peru and Bolivia lose territory to Chile
12,000 BC	1200 BC 200 BC – 1200 AD	1400 – 1532 1530	1821 1825 1830 1879 – 83 1941
The first people reach South America	The Tiahuanaco culture flourishes in Bolivia	The Inca empire is at its peak	Peru, Bolivia and Ecuador gain independence	Peru and Ecuador go to war over a border dispute

◀ *A sniffer dog checks suitcases for drugs. All three countries have problems with drug trafficking.*

President can stand for re-election immediately – which is not the case in Ecuador or Bolivia. There is also a single 120-seat chamber. Voting in elections is compulsory. Any eligible person who does not vote is fined.

Bolivia effectively has two capital cities. Congress is based in La Paz, while the legal capital is Sucre. Under the Constitution of 1967, the President is elected for a four-year term. Congress consists of two chambers: the Senate with 27 seats and the Chamber of Deputies with 130.

▼ *President Fujimori of Peru celebrates his election for a second five-year term in 1995.*

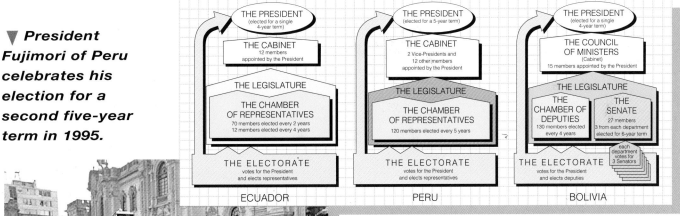

ECUADOR

THE PRESIDENT
(elected for a single 4-year term)

THE CABINET
12 members
appointed by the President

THE LEGISLATURE

THE CHAMBER OF REPRESENTATIVES
70 members elected every 2 years
12 members elected every 4 years

THE ELECTORATE
votes for the President
and elects representatives

PERU

THE PRESIDENT
(elected for a 5-year term)

THE CABINET
2 Vice-Presidents and
12 other members
appointed by the President

THE LEGISLATURE

THE CHAMBER OF REPRESENTATIVES
120 members elected every 5 years

THE ELECTORATE
votes for the President
and elects representatives

BOLIVIA

THE PRESIDENT
(elected for a single 4-year term)

THE COUNCIL OF MINISTERS
(Cabinet)
15 members appointed by the President

THE LEGISLATURE

THE CHAMBER OF DEPUTIES
130 members elected every 4 years

THE SENATE
27 members
3 from each department elected for 6-year term

each department votes for 3 Senators

THE ELECTORATE
votes for the President
and elects deputies

In all three countries, the electors have to be at least 18-years old. However, in Bolivia people who are not married cannot vote until they are 21.

All three countries have suffered from terrorist activity, when normal life was disrupted by bombings, killings and kidnappings. However, Peru's Sendero Luminoso, the most feared terrorist group, has now almost ceased its activities.

FOOD AND FARMING

Agriculture employs more than a third of the working populations of Peru and Ecuador, and 62% of Bolivia's workforce. It also makes an important contibution to the countries' economies, earning hundreds of millions of dollars a year. However, many farmers have small plots and produce just enough food to feed their families; this is known as SUBSISTENCE FARMING.

Most of the land in the region is not suitable for the cultivation of crops. Only 3% of the total land area of Peru and Bolivia is under cultivation, compared with 9% in Ecuador, but IRRIGATION and the use of the rainforest mean that these figures may rise.

The most intensively farmed areas are the coastal strips of Ecuador and Peru. Large areas of Ecuador's Pacific coastal plains have been drained and grow the bulk of the country's export crops, of which the most important are bananas, coffee, cocoa,

▶ *Thousands of small fish are caught in Lake Titicaca and dried in the sun.*

▲ *Bananas are an important crop in the region. Here, they are being loaded for transport at Riberalta, Bolivia.*

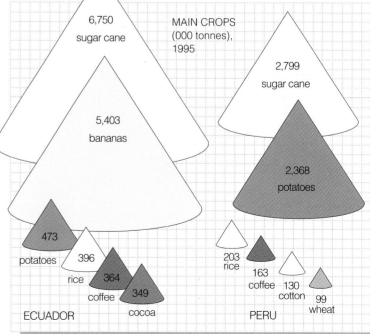

MAIN CROPS (000 tonnes), 1995

ECUADOR
- 6,750 sugar cane
- 5,403 bananas
- 473 potatoes
- 396 rice
- 364 coffee
- 349 cocoa

PERU
- 2,799 sugar cane
- 2,368 potatoes
- 203 rice
- 163 coffee
- 130 cotton
- 99 wheat

rice and sugar. Ecuador is the world's largest exporter of bananas, which earned US$ 650 million in export income in 1994. Along Peru's coastal desert, 'high-tech' irrigation techniques are used and the percentage of irrigated land has grown from 3.73% in 1975 to 4.15% in 1993. The principal crops here are cotton, sugar, asparagus and fruit.

In the Andes, most farming consists of tiny farm plots, worked by families. Many of the techniques used by subsistence farmers have changed little for hundreds of years. The main crops are potatoes, maize and beans, together with cereals cultivated since Inca times, such as quinoa and kiwicha.

The rainforested eastern sectors of all three countries have very low population densities and limited agriculture. But these are the areas of the greatest agricultural potential. Around half of the region's total territory is covered by lowland rainforest, where conditions are excellent for growing crops such as tea, coffee and cocoa. The

lack of good transport routes has meant that until recently only small quantities of these crops were cultivated. Bolivia has the most developed agriculture in the eastern sector, while cattle ranching has led to a rapid rise in the country's beef exports, especially to Brazil.

The region has enormous potential in terms of timber production, as more than half the total land area is covered by forest or woodland. The Amazon basin is a rich source of hardwoods such as cedar and

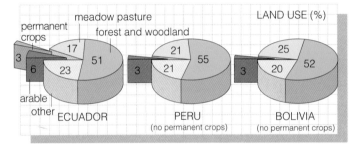

▼ *A field of barley being harvested by hand near Huaraz, Peru. Barley was one of the crops introduced by the Spanish after they conquered the Inca empire.*

mahogany. Other products include rubber and quinine (used in the treatment of malaria). Bolivia earned US$ 46 million from exports of timber in 1992, while Ecuador's exports accounted for US$ 16.5 million in 1993. Most of the 7.5 million cubic metres of timber harvested in Peru in 1991 were used for firewood or making charcoal. Only a small proportion was sawn into planks.

The fishing industries of Peru and Ecuador are also important. The cold Humboldt current that sweeps up Peru's coastline creates ideal conditions for fish to breed, although every few years this is replaced by a warm ocean current, and the fish stocks fall to almost nothing. However, in good years Peru is second only to China in terms of the size of its fish catch. Anchovies are the main type of fish caught. These and other small fish are chiefly used

◄ *In the Andes, fresh produce is sold in markets such as this one in the village of Pizac, near Cuzco, in Peru.*

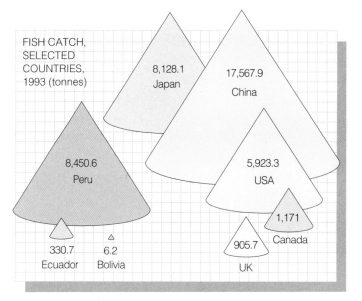

FISH CATCH, SELECTED COUNTRIES, 1993 (tonnes)

8,128.1 Japan

17,567.9 China

8,450.6 Peru

5,923.3 USA

330.7 Ecuador

6.2 Bolivia

1,171 Canada

905.7 UK

▼ *A young man sprays a crop of flowers with pesticide. Cut flowers from Ecuador and Peru are exported to the USA and beyond. This is a thriving industry.*

to produce fishmeal. In 1994, the country's fishmeal exports were worth US$ 709 million, making it Peru's second most important export, after copper.

Ecuador is South America's largest producer of shrimps and ranks second in the world. The shrimps are cultivated in lagoons cut out of the MANGROVE forests that line the coast. Shrimps are one of Ecuador's three main exports, along with oil and bananas. In 1994, the country's shrimp exports reached a new record of US$ 539 million.

As a landlocked country, Bolivia has a small fishing industry, restricted to its rivers and lakes. Lake Titicaca is an important natural fishery and there are also commercial trout farms here. Most of Bolivia's fish catch is for local consumption.

The staple foods of the local population are potatoes, rice and maize. Meat such as beef and pork are not regular parts of the general diet, but they are popular on feast days and holidays.

KEY FACTS

● 17% of Ecuador's total export income comes from bananas and 16% from shrimps.
● Cut flower exports earned US$ 54.5 million for Ecuador in 1994.
● Bolivia is the world's second largest exporter of Brazil nuts (after Brazil), producing 5,500 tonnes in 1991.
● More than 300 types of potato are grown in the Andes. Some grow at altitudes over 4,000 metres.
● Guinea pigs are a major source of protein for rural Andean families.

TRADE AND INDUSTRY

At the end of the Second World War in 1945, all three countries had economies based on PRIMARY PRODUCTS (raw materials such as minerals and agricultural produce). These continue to be the mainstay of the three economies, but now there are also industries to process these raw materials. In addition, many other industries have been set up to help reduce the countries' reliance on expensive imports, which include everything from shoes and cars to electronics.

ECUADOR

Ecuador relies on three main exports – oil, bananas and shrimps. They accounted for 70% of exports in 1994. This makes the country vulnerable, as the world prices that are paid for these commodities can change at any time.

Since 1965, industrialization has taken off. The first industries to be set up in the country included food processing and textiles, taking advantage of Ecuador's excellent agricultural production. In 1993, the food, drink and tobacco industries still dominated the manufacturing sector of the economy, accounting for 62% of the total value of this sector.

During the 1990s, most industrial growth has been in the manufacture of chemicals, machinery and paper, and the processing of wood products. However, manufacturing exports remain small in comparison with other sectors of Ecuador's economy.

▲ **The Otovalan Indians of Ecuador produce high-quality handicrafts, selling them in stores such as this one, which can be found all over Ecuador. Some items are exported.**

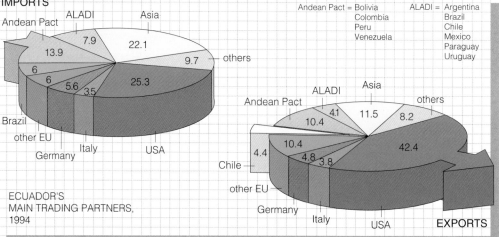

IMPORTS

Andean Pact — ALADI — Asia — 7.9 — 22.1 — 9.7 — others
13.9
6
6 — 5.6 — 3.5 — 25.3
Brazil
other EU
Germany — Italy — USA

Andean Pact = Bolivia, Colombia, Peru, Venezuela

ALADI = Argentina, Brazil, Chile, Mexico, Paraguay, Uruguay

ECUADOR'S MAIN TRADING PARTNERS, 1994

Andean Pact — ALADI — Asia — others
10.4 — 4.1 — 11.5 — 8.2
Chile — 4.4 — 10.4 — 4.8 — 3.8 — 42.4
other EU
Germany — Italy — USA — EXPORTS

PERU

Peru has one of the fastest growing economies in Latin America. There has been steady growth since 1990, and in 1994 the economy grew by 8.6%. This compares with growth of 3.9% in Ecuador.

Today, Peru is modernizing its industries. It is also looking more towards the booming Asian countries on the far side of the Pacific as its future trading partners.

As with many other South American countries, Peru depends to a large extent on its natural resources to earn foreign income. For example, mineral exports were worth US$ 1.86 billion in 1994: 40.8% of total export income. One of the other major resources is fish for the fishmeal industry. But this industry is vulnerable to climatic changes, which can bring dramatic declines in the fish catch.

Peru's main industries are the mining of metals, petroleum, fishing, textiles, clothing, food processing, vehicle assembly, cement, steel and ship-building. Since 1979, the

▲ *High-grade cotton grown on Peru's coastal strip provides one of the main raw materials for the textile industry.*

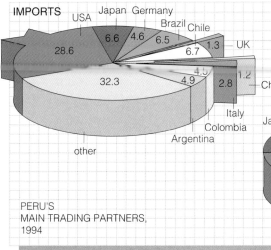

IMPORTS
USA Japan Germany
Brazil Chile
6.6 4.6 6.5
6.7 1.3 — UK
28.6
4.5 1.2
32.3 4.9 2.8 — China
Italy
Colombia
Argentina
other
PERU'S MAIN TRADING PARTNERS, 1994

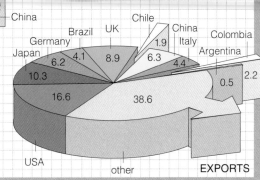

Chile
Brazil UK China Colombia
Germany 1.9 Italy Argentina
Japan 6.2 4.1 8.9 6.3 4.4
10.3 0.5 2.2
16.6 38.6
USA
other EXPORTS

▲ *Thousands of people work at the copper, silver and lead smelting plant at La Oroya in the Peruvian Andes.*

fastest growing industries have been beverages (up by more than 220%), non-metallic minerals (up 158%) and non-industrial chemicals (up 102%).

BOLIVIA

Bolivia is the least industrially developed of all three countries. It relies heavily on mining and minerals such as tin, gold and antimony, which earned 39% of its export income in 1994. Agricultural exports are also important, with soya beans alone accounting for another 11% of exports.

A new and significant export is natural gas, which is piped to Argentina and Brazil. Argentina is the main customer for the gas, which is fed through a 526-kilometre pipeline. This export was worth around US$ 96 million in 1994. A new 2,233-kilometre pipeline is also being built from Bolivia to the State of

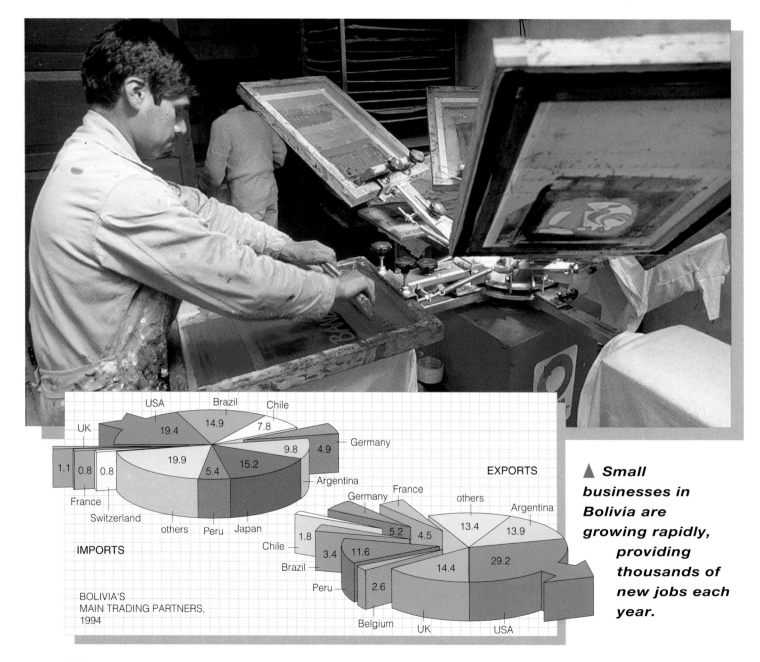

BOLIVIA'S MAIN TRADING PARTNERS, 1994

IMPORTS
USA 19.4, Brazil 14.9, Chile 7.8, Germany 4.9, Argentina 15.2, Japan 5.4, Peru 19.9, others, Switzerland, France 0.8, 0.8, UK 1.1, Germany 9.8

EXPORTS
Argentina 13.9, others 13.4, France 4.5, Germany 5.2, Chile 1.8, Brazil 3.4, Peru 11.6, Belgium 2.6, UK 14.4, USA 29.2

▲ *Small businesses in Bolivia are growing rapidly, providing thousands of new jobs each year.*

KEY FACTS

● Authentic Panama hats are made in Cuenca, Ecuador – not in Panama. They are chiefly exported to the USA and Central American countries.

● Ecuador earned US$ 1,185 million from the export of crude oil in 1995.

● In 1993, Ecuador earned US$ 230 million from tourism, making it the country's fourth largest earner of foreign currency.

● Peru's food industry is dominated by only two companies, La Fabril and the Gloria Group.

● Between 1991 and 1995, US$ 400 million was spent on modernizing Peru's fishing fleet.

● Bolivia is the world's fifth largest producer of tin.

▼ *All three countries have oil industries. This is the base camp for an oil operation in the Amazon basin.*

São Paulo in Brazil, to start exporting natural gas in 1998.

Manufacturing industries grew slowly in the 40 years after the Second World War. But since 1984 there has been more rapid growth, especially in the food, drinks, tobacco and textile industries, which have been responsible for 60% of the new growth. However, in an attempt to cut costs, more than a third of Bolivia's manufacturing work-force lost their jobs between 1984 and 1996.

An important new development is the creation and support of 'micro industries'. This involves thousands of small businesses producing high-value products. The most successful of these, so far, has been jewellery. Hundreds of small jewellery businesses had a combined export income of more than US$ 120 million in 1994: 11% of the country's total.

TRANSPORT

The varied terrain of Ecuador, Peru and Bolivia makes communications difficult. The Andes are a formidable barrier between the coastal strips and the eastern lowlands in Peru and Ecuador. This has led to distinct differences in transport systems between various areas in all three countries.

The best road networks are along the coastal strips of Ecuador and Peru. Excellent paved roads, including the pan-American highway, run north–south along the coast, linking Guayaquil and places

▼ Buses in La Paz and other major cities are plentiful and cheap to use. The fares are kept low, so that poorer people can afford to travel to work or market.

KEY FACTS

● According to local reports, runners could carry a message the length of the Inca empire (2,400 kilometres) in 5–10 days.
● La Paz has the world's highest commercial airport, at a height of 4,018 metres.
● Ecuador has only 965 kilometres of railway track, compared with 1,801 kilometres in Peru and 3,684 kilometres in Bolivia.
● The only way to move heavy goods from Iquitos in the Peruvian Amazon to the port of Callao (1,010 kilometres by air) is overland and via the Panama Canal, a trip of 11,250 kilometres.

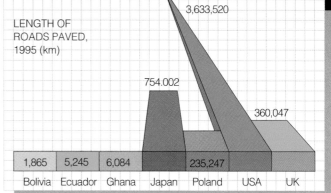

LENGTH OF ROADS PAVED, 1995 (km)

Bolivia	Ecuador	Ghana	Japan	Poland	USA	UK
1,865	5,245	6,084	754.002	235,247	3,633,520	360,047

further north to Lima, and towns as far south as Arequipa. However, only a limited number of roads lead from the coast up over mountain passes into the Andes.

The road system in the Andes is poor and the majority of roads are unpaved. The main forms of transport for ordinary people are train and bus, which are often overcrowded. The road system in the eastern lowlands is very limited. Only a few roads are usable all year round, because of the heavy rainfall here.

The railway systems of all three countries are becoming less important for moving raw materials, such as minerals and agricultural produce. In Ecuador, only 33,694 tonnes of rail freight were carried in 1993. Trains and

◀ *Peru has an impressive network of more than 50 airports. Many are at altitudes of more than 3,000 metres. This is Arequipa airport, where thousands of tourists arrive every year.*

railway lines are generally old and in a poor state of repair.

Because of the difficult terrain, air travel is extremely important in all three countries. There are more than 50 airports in Peru, while both Quito and La Paz airports handle large amounts of air cargo.

In the eastern sectors of all three countries, the rivers, especially the tributaries of the Amazon, provide the most important transport system. All the rivers in this area flow away from the capital cities and towards the Atlantic.

Peru has 21 ports through which the bulk of its produce is exported. Ecuador has four main ports and another two deep-water terminals for oil tankers. However, the port of Guayquil handles 81% of all non-oil exports. Bolivia has access to sea ports only via other countries.

▶ *In the remoter parts of the Andes, people often have to carry goods and basic items themselves, or use pack animals. These Canari Indians are taking fodder collected in the mountains back to their animals at home.*

THE ENVIRONMENT

Ecuador, Peru and Bolivia have a wide range of environments, ranging from deserts to snow-capped peaks, and from lowland rainforests to high altiplano grasslands. Each type of environment faces its own particular problems.

Close to the big cities and industrial complexes, air pollution has become a serious problem. Vehicles and factories in

▲ Vicuña are the rarest of the four species of camelids that inhabit the Andes (the others are llama, alpaca and guanaco). These vicuña are protected in a national reserve in southern Peru.

cities like La Paz, Quito and Cuzco all produce large quantities of pollutants. These cities are also ringed by mountains, so the pollution cannot disperse easily, but tends to build up instead. This has caused serious health problems. Coastal cities are also polluted by emissions from vehicles and from industries such as metal-smelting and fish-processing. Water contamination is a serious problem, too — the water from Lima's main river, the Rimac, is undrinkable.

Some of the farming methods employed in all three countries are also affecting local environments. Along Peru's coastal strip, industrial farming techniques include irrigation and high chemical imputs. But intensive agriculture is rapidly exhausting the soils, while the chemical run-off is

KEY FACTS

● Peru's Manu National Park covers 1.5 million hectares (half the size of Switzerland). In one 5-hectare plot, scientists have found 10% of all the world's species of birds and 1,000 different types of plants.
● One metal smelter at La Oroya in the Peruvian Andes has contaminated 700,000 hectares of farmland with toxic pollutants over the last 30 years.
● 95% of Ecuador's coastal forests have been destroyed since Europeans arrived there.

◀ *Agriculture and the timber industry have led to deforestation in the rainforest.*

▼ *Tree-planting in some Peruvian reserves helps replace forest and protect against soil erosion.*

DEFORESTATION, 1981–90
(% of land deforested)

1.2	Mexico
3.3	Bangladesh
1.3	Ghana
0.4	Peru
0.1	USA
0	Japan

polluting rivers and drinking water. Meanwhile, although Peru is today the world's second largest fishing nation, over-fishing means that, at current rates, the fish stocks off the coast may be reduced to almost nothing in only a few years' time.

Ecuador's coastal farmlands have also suffered the effects of industrial farming techniques. Moreover, intensive shrimp farming here has destroyed thousands of

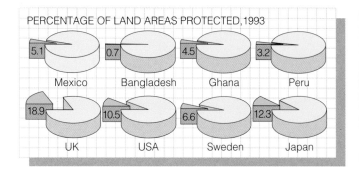

PERCENTAGE OF LAND AREAS PROTECTED, 1993

5.1 Mexico	0.7 Bangladesh	4.5 Ghana	3.2 Peru
18.9 UK	10.5 USA	6.6 Sweden	12.3 Japan

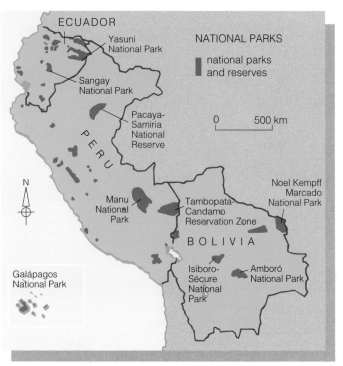

ECUADOR

Yasuni National Park

Sangay National Park

Pacaya-Samiria National Reserve

PERU

Manu National Park

Tambopata-Candamo Reservation Zone

Noel Kempff Marcado National Park

BOLIVIA

Isiboro-Sécure National Park

Amboró National Park

Galápagos National Park

NATIONAL PARKS

■ national parks and reserves

0   500 km

N

hectares of mangrove forest since the early 1980s – these were once the breeding grounds of important commercial fish.

The rainforested lowlands in the east of the region have so far suffered less, although the expansion of farming (such as cattle ranches in Bolivia) is having an impact. Moreover, the discovery of oil in the Ecuadorean rainforest (in 1972) has led to serious river pollution in an area that contains indigenous people and some of the world's rarest animal and plant species. It is feared that similar problems will occur when new Peruvian and Bolivian oil and natural gas fields are developed.

Many people are aware of the environmental problems facing all three countries and are campaigning to reduce pollution and to protect areas of great biological importance. In some cases, local environmental groups have been successful in this. For example, in the early 1990s local and international pressure led to the setting up of the Biosphere Reserve of Beni and Yacuma Regional Park, covering a combined area of 685,000 hectares in Bolivia.

Governments have a good reason to protect areas of wilderness, as they attract

◀ *An iguana, with a small lizard climbing over it, basks on the rocks of one of the Galápagos Islands.*

▶ *A condor glides over the Colca Canyon in Peru. Condors are the heaviest of all birds of prey and can have a wing span of more than 3 metres. These birds are most often seen in the high Andes, but they may also fly along canyons to the coast in search of food.*

tourists from all over the world, who contribute millions of dollars to the economy. However, tourism can pose problems. For example, the Galápagos Islands are home to many rare species of plants and animals. But the estimated 60,000 visitors a year are causing problems for the islands' fragile environment. There have also been calls to build a new airport here, which would help the economy but destroy part of the environment. The Ecuadorean government has controlled development on the islands so far, but some newly arrived islanders want more tourist facilities to be built. In 1994, angry islanders deliberately started fires in the Galápagos and around 10,000 hectares of land on Isla Isabella were destroyed.

THE FUTURE

Ecuador, Peru and Bolivia all have great potential for the future. They are rich in natural resources. They also have young populations and are enjoying a period of political stability. At the same time, their economies are growing and they are ideally placed to develop trade links with the strong economies of Asian countries such as Japan, South Korea and Malaysia. However, they still face many challenges.

Despite their natural wealth, the three countries have serious social problems. The rural populations of Peru and Bolivia, in particular, experience some of the worst living conditions in South America. However, there have been improvements – for example, life expectancy in Ecuador increased by 11 years between 1960 and 1992.

▲ *President Fujimori of Peru has promised better school facilities, such as computers, to help prepare young people for new types of jobs.*

One major problem facing all three countries is how to provide employment for their growing populations. In Peru, education has become a top priority, and expenditure on education doubled between 1990 and 1995. With a highly educated workforce, Peru should be able to create large numbers of skilled jobs in manufacturing and processing. Meanwhile, in Bolivia the government is supporting

KEY FACTS

● In 1993, international debts totalled US$ 22.2 billion in Peru, US$ 13.2 billion in Ecuador and US$ 4.1 billion in Bolivia.
● In 1993–95, the proportion of people aged under 15 was 35% in Ecuador, 36% in Peru and 39% in Bolivia.

▶ *Students at La Paz University have decorated the walls of their campus with artwork representing the history and political struggles of Bolivia.*

◀ *In Quito, the capital of Ecuador, the commercial sector of the city has grown in the last few years.*

thousands of small businesses which are creating new jobs and wealth. Ecuador is continuing to develop processing industries to take advantage of its huge natural wealth.

Some of the problems facing the region are drug trafficking, the size of the international debts owed by each country, and the large gap between the rich and the poor. In addition, there are environmental problems, such as over-fishing, air and water pollution and the continuing destruction of rainforests.

However, the future for this varied region could be very bright. If people's living standards continue to improve, if natural resources are wisely managed and if challenges such as drug trafficking and pollution are confronted, a better and more secure future should be possible for all.

FURTHER INFORMATION

● ACTION AID EDUCATION DEPARTMENT
Hamlyn House, MacDonald Road, Archway,
London NW19 5PG
Produces publications and audio-visual material on Peru and Bolivia, including material focusing on children.
● HISPANIC AND LUSO BRAZILIAN
COUNCIL
Canning House, 2 Belgrave Square,
London SW1X 8PJ
Has an excellent library on South America.
● OXFAM EDUCATION DEPARTMENT
274 Banbury Road, Oxford OX2 7DX
Produces special education packs, plus videos, slide sets and leaflets, on all three countries.

BOOKS ABOUT THE REGION
● *Peru: A Study of an Economically Developing Country,* Edward Parker, Wayland 1996 (age 11–14)
● *Peru and the Andean Countries,* Chantal Deltenre and Martine Noblet, Barron's 1995 (age 9–12)
● *South America,* Ewan McLeish, Wayland 1996 (age 9–12)
● *World in View: Ecuador, Peru and Bolivia,* Marion Morrison, Heinemann Children's Reference 1991 (age 11–14)

GLOSSARY

ALTIPLANO
A Spanish word for 'high plain'. It is used to describe the large expanse of level land in the Andes region.

DEFORESTATION
The clearing of trees, either so they can be used as fuel, etc., or so that the land can be used for a different purpose, such as farming.

DEMOCRACY
A country which is governed by politicians elected by the people of that country.

EL NIÑO
A warm ocean current that, once every five to ten years, replaces the cold current off the coast of Peru and Ecuador, causing torrential rains to fall over desert lands.

FIESTA
The Spanish word for party or celebration.

FISHMEAL
Dried ground fish that is used for pet food or as a fertilizer.

FOSSIL FUELS
These include fuels such as coal, oil and gas which are composed of the fossilized remains of plants.

GARÚA
A cool, damp fog that hangs over much of the coast of Peru between April and November.

GEOLOGICAL FAULT
A line of weakness in the earth's crust, caused by violent movement deep inside the earth over millions of years. Volcanoes and earthquakes are frequently associated with these areas.

GUANO
An accumulation of bird droppings, rich in nitrates and phosphates, used as a fertilizer.

INDIGENOUS
The original inhabitants of a particular region.

IRRIGATION
An artificial water supply for growing crops, for example using water channels.

MANGROVE
Tropical trees that only grow in wet areas. They have distinctive roots which grow out of the water.

MESTIZO
A person of mixed ancestry, who is partly native Ecuadorean, Peruvian or Bolivian, and partly European.

OASIS
A fertile spot in a desert where water can be found.

PACHA MANCA
A Quechua (Inca) word meaning an oven in the ground. Typically, rocks are heated over a fire; then food is placed on the rocks, covered with earth and left to cook for several hours.

PRIMARY PRODUCTS
Things produced that have not yet been processed by industry. They include all types of farm produce, and products of mining and forestry.

SUBSISTENCE FARMING
A form of livelihood in which someone produces only enough food for his or her family to eat.

TRIBUTARY
A stream or river that flows into a larger river or lake.